KITTENS

by
Pat Taylor

Hamlyn
London·New York·Sydney·Toronto

PHOTO ACKNOWLEDGEMENTS

Barnaby's Picture Library 18, 22tr, 42bl; Camera Clix Inc. 4; Camera Press Ltd. 29, 36, 38, 42r; Central Press Photos Ltd. 21; Will Green 16, 19, 22br, 23l, 23r, 24r, 35tr, 47tl, 47tr, 47b, 51, 54, 57bl; VK Guy 13; Paul Kaye 8, 12; Tierbilder Okapia 50l; PAF International endpapers; Photo Researchers 10tl, 30, 33, 40, 53; Pictorial Press 9, 10tr, 11, 14t, 14br, 15, 26, 27, 31, 34, 35tl, 43, 55, 57t, 57br, 60, 61; Popperfoto 10b, 17, 25, 32, 52; Rex Features 20, 24l, 28, 35b, 39, 46, 48b, 49, 50r, 58; Syndication International cover, 22l, 37, 44, 45, 48t; Sally Anne Thompson 14bl, 41, 56, 59; John Topham Ltd. 42tl.

First Published 1970
Second Impression 1971

Published by the Hamlyn Publishing Group Limited
London · New York · Sydney · Toronto
Hamlyn House, Feltham, Middlesex, England
© The Hamlyn Publishing Group Limited, 1970
Printed in Canary Islands (Spain) by
Litografia A. Romero, S.A., Santa Cruz de Tenerife
ISBN 0 600 34814 8

CONTENTS

A KITTEN IS BORN

No baby creature in the whole world is as lovable as a kitten. All baby animals are fascinating, it's true. But who wants to cuddle a baby snake? You'd have to sit on an iceberg to play with a young penguin, or climb a mountain to see a newly-hatched eagle. But a kitten can be born in your own home, where you can watch it, and, when it's old enough, you can have more fun playing with it than with a barrelful of monkeys!

If you're lucky enough to have kittens born in your own home, make sure you have the right place for them. What the mother cat needs is a warm nest in a dark, quiet place. A box measuring one and a half feet each way, with sides a foot high, makes a good bed. Newspaper torn into strips, straw or soft cloth should be put in the bottom. Then you have to find the right place for the bed. If the mother cat doesn't like the place you've chosen, she'll find a better one of her own.

Cats very rarely need help when the kittens are being born. They prefer to be left alone. But if they do seem to need attention, that's best left to a veterinarian.

Newborn kittens are quite weak, and are both blind and deaf. They shouldn't be touched at all, because this upsets the mother cat. In fact, some cats will disown or ignore their kittens if people touch them, and the kittens will die of neglect.

But the mother cat won't mind if you just watch them for a bit. You'll hear the kittens making sad, lost little miaows as they try to crawl or stagger about the nest. And you'll see their mother gather them up and bring them back to nestle against her if they can't find their own way back to her.

The mother cat lies on her side, curving her body round the kittens to warm them and stop them wandering. They soon settle down to drinking her milk and sleeping.

Opposite page: A kitten nestled against his mother while being groomed is oblivious to the world around him.

Above: Abyssinian mother and kitten. They're more friendly than most cats and make very good pets.

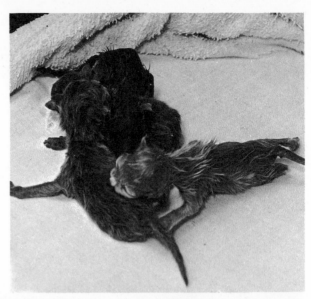

Opposite page, top left: A kitten suckling from its mother.
Opposite page, top right: These kittens were photographed only
six minutes after birth. Their coats are still wet.
At left and above: If a kitten runs away, mother carries him
home. And if he won't be still, she holds him back.

Most mother cats are the same—they always seem to be washing their offspring. Human children come in for a lot of washing, but kittens seem to get more than their share. This is not just to clean them. When the mother licks her kittens their blood circulates, keeping them warm and healthy.

Sometimes—not at all often—a mother cat dies when her kittens are born. Or she may disown her kittens and push them out of the nest. It's possible to raise these orphans by bottle feeding them until they're bigger—about three or four weeks old. But this is a big job. At first they'll need feeding every two hours, night and day! So it's not the kind of job for a young child to take on.

The best thing to do for orphan kittens is to find them a new mother—one who has milk for them, of course. She could be one who has lost all or most of her own kittens. There's a little trick you can play on her, so that she'll take to the kittens at first. Give her a good rub with a soft cloth and then rub the kittens with it. What you're doing is rubbing her smell on to them. Then they seem familiar to her, and she'll settle down and look after them.

Ordinarily, kittens are completely looked after by their mothers for their first three

11

or four weeks. When their milk teeth come through, you can start feeding them on a little extra milk. You will learn more about feeding in the next chapter.

No kitten should leave its mother until it's about eight weeks old. By that time it will be fully weaned, have its first set of teeth, and be able to eat solid foods. Also, mother cats train their kittens in a lot of ways. One of the most important things they learn is to use a toilet pan. The best pan is low and flat, with sides high enough to keep the contents in. It can be filled with sand or other clean material. Pet shops sell a synthetic sand-like material for cat pans, which kills any smell there might be. The pan should be cleaned at least twice a week. Wash the pan with soap and hot water, and rinse it well before refilling it with fresh material. Don't use detergent to clean it–the smell bothers cats' noses.

Most of us don't have kittens born in our own home, but choose one from elsewhere. It's very important to make the right choice, and to be sure that it's a kitten you'll still love when it grows up to be a *cat*.

First, make sure that the kittens you look at are old enough to be taken away. Then make sure that they're *all* healthy. If one kitten in a litter looks sick, while the others are all right, it's still better to leave them all. The healthy-looking ones could have caught cat flu or some other ailment, though it might not show until later.

What does a healthy kitten look like? He has bright, clear eyes–not at all runny. His ears are clean and don't smell. He should have a healthy skin, with no sores or rough spots. You can feel for these by stroking him gently. Testing a kitten's stomach is also important. A healthy stomach will feel firm and a bit rubbery. If it feels too soft or very hard, don't choose that kitten.

Suppose you're looking at a litter of lovely kittens, all bursting with health. You will probably like them all–who wouldn't? But which is the best? Don't choose entirely on the colour of his coat, because that could change as he grows up. It's difficult to know what each kitten is really like, just from watching them for a few minutes. The one who's having a kip when you first see it isn't necessarily a dozey one. Perhaps he's been playing for hours and is taking forty winks to restore his energy!

One of the first things you'll learn about your own kitten, when you come to know him, is that he's different from any other kitten or cat. Don't make the mistake of thinking that all kittens are the same–they do have different personalities, likes and dislikes just like people.

But since it takes a while to know a kitten, you really have to take pot luck in choosing. There are one or two things you can spot almost at once. Usually there's a 'boss' kitten. He or she will be the one who pushes the others out of the way to get to the food first. If there's a favourite, warm corner in the nest, he'll be the one to make sure he gets it. The boss kitten is one with a mind of his own, who will grow up having a way of his own, no matter what *you* want. He's not usually the cuddly kind who likes lots of petting and fussing.

A nervous kitten is not the best choice. If you approach a kitten quietly, and talk to him for a bit before trying to touch him or pick him up, he shouldn't be afraid. But the kitten who raises his fur, spits or backs away from you is a nervous one.

Everyone likes a playful kitten. Once the kittens are used to you, get them to play. A bit of paper on a string is a good toy. Playful kittens will rush at it, bat it about, try to eat it or drag it away. Having watched them a while, you'll probably find you like one better than the others–and he'll be your choice.

Where do you look for kittens? First, it depends on what kind of kitten you want. If you want a particular breed–a Siamese or a Red Tabby or a Blue Burmese or

whatever—you must find someone who breeds them. Pedigree cats can be very beautiful indeed. They're also expensive. And on the whole they don't make any better—or worse—pets than ordinary kittens and cats. If you want a kitten just as a pet, as a nice animal to have in your home, then ordinary kittens are best. In fact, there are always more kittens needing homes than there are homes for them. You'll find kittens advertised in local newspapers, or a friend may have some to give away; you may get them free from a nearby animal welfare society, or buy them in a pet shop.

When you've found your kitten, you have to get him home. You should realise that he'll be nervous about being taken away from his mother and home. So it's best to take him in a box or cat basket. Make sure it's comfortable for him. Don't joggle him about any more than you can help, and make the journey as short as possible.

When you've got him home, don't expect him to start playing with you at once, because he'll be feeling a bit lost and upset. Also, he'll want to find out all about his new home. The best thing is to keep him in one room. Stay and talk to him, but let him roam about and explore. Make sure he has a sand box, somewhere to sleep, and a bowl

of warm milk or water. Pat him and make a fuss of him if he wants it, but otherwise leave him alone. Don't let too many people fuss over him at first—that's sure to make him feel nervous and frightened.

His sleeping place should be warm and away from draughts. If he doesn't like the place you choose for him, he'll find one of his own, and that might not be a good choice from *your* point of view. Most people aren't too happy if their kitten decides to sleep in the sideboard or in Dad's favourite armchair! Until he gets used to being without his mother, he'll probably like having a hot water bottle in his basket. And if he cries at night, there's a good way of getting him off to sleep. Wrap a clock in a piece of cloth and put it beside him. The ticking sound will soon comfort him to sleep—it reminds him of his mother's heartbeat. But if you do, please remember to turn off any alarm bell on the clock. He'd get an awful shock if that went off under his ear!

When he's happy in the first room you show him, you can take him to explore other parts of the house. And until he's quite settled down and is happy with you and your home, keep him indoors. Otherwise he might run or wander away.

GROWING UP

Kittens grow up very rapidly, and are adult cats by the age of six months for female cats and about nine months for toms. They will live with you, as pleasing and satisfying pets, for many happy years. But their lives will be shortened, and their health will be poor, if they aren't fed properly right from the start.

It's not true that kittens and cats need only a very simple diet—just fish and meat. It's best to give them a wide range of foods, to make sure they get all the vitamins and minerals they need to grow up healthy.

Cats which run wild eat mice and rats, birds, fish and insects. They also eat grass and other green shoots and some vegetables. In this way they make sure of supplying their bodies with all the food elements they need. Pet cats and kittens don't get the same chances to find their own food. It's up to their owners to make sure that they get everything they need to stay strong and healthy.

For his first three or four weeks of life, your kitten's needs are supplied by his mother's milk. Then his milk teeth come through, and you can start weaning him. First, teach him to drink milk from a saucer. This can be cow's milk but, if it gives him diarrhoea, try half evaporated milk and half water—always served at room temperature.

Some kittens learn to lap milk from a saucer with no trouble at all. Others need to be shown how—but not by having their noses pushed in it. The best way is to dip your finger in the milk, and dab it on the kitten's chin. He'll lick it off, and look for more. Soon he'll be licking the milk from your finger. Then you can draw him up to the saucer by putting your finger in the milk. He'll quickly discover the real source of supply and how to lap milk from the saucer.

To begin with, he won't want much milk, because his mother will still be feeding him. Give him tiny amounts about four times a day. When he's happy with that, start him on strained meats such as baby food. Then, as his teeth grow, give him ordinary meat chopped fine enough so that he can chew it easily. Soft-boiled egg mixed with his food is very good at this stage, too.

Quite tiny amounts of food are needed to begin with. For a month-old kitten, one

19

The kitten playing on the watering can is a real tabby.

ounce of food, including milk, is enough for one day. At two months, he should be fed two ounces a day, at three months three ounces. His diet should be half meat, one quarter milk, and one quarter egg. Never forget to keep a bowl of water handy—some cats don't like milk after their babyhood. When your kitten grows to a cat, he'll weigh ten to twelve pounds. At that weight he should get about half a pound of food per day, split up into three or four feeds. This should include meat, fish, eggs, milk, vegetables and cheese. It's not necessary to feed something of everything every day, but the more variety you can give, the better. No one food—and that includes tinned pet foods—can supply all his needs. And if you start him off on just one type of food, he may not want to eat anything else. So keep up the variety, and don't overfeed.

Have you ever watched a cat stalking a bird and thought how very much like a wild creature he was? Even a fluffy kitten pouncing on a toy mouse can look very much like his wild ancestors. In fact, all cats, domestic and wild, are very similar in build and appearance. Size is the main difference. Tame cats can go feral—return to the wild—while the cubs of wild cats like lions and cheetahs can be tamed.

The Scottish wild cat is a real wild cat, never having been domesticated. He looks much like a domestic tabby cat, but his ears lie flat against his head and he is larger and heavier. Even our domestic cats, which probably originated on the African continent, and have none of the Scottish wild cat blood in them, are so like the wild cat that they can cross breed and produce kittens.

To understand your kitten, it helps to know how he's built, and what his natural needs and abilities are.

Cats are really nocturnal, or night animals. You can tell this from their eyesight, which is very good in the dark. This is for two reasons. First, the iris—the dark centre of the eye—can open very wide to let in a lot of light. Second, there is a reflecting layer,

the tapetum, in the back of the eye. This tapetum collects and concentrates the light on the retina, where it is needed. When you see your kitten's eyes glow in the dark, it's the light reflected from the tapetum that you're seeing.

Kittens see much better in the dark than humans but ordinarily their eyesight isn't as clear; to see clearly they have to be five times closer than humans do. However, their eyes can see any movement quicker than you can.

Everything about your kitten's body makes him a perfect hunter. His hearing, for instance, is very good indeed. In the low frequencies of sound his hearing is about the same as yours. But in the higher frequencies his ears are much better, and he can hear sounds that you can't. The shape of his ears is very helpful, too. They stand up and catch sound. There are twenty-seven muscles in each ear, so he can swivel them to scoop up sounds coming from different directions.

Kittens use their tongues for more than eating or drinking. If your kitten licks your hand—which is a way he has of showing affection—you'll feel that the tongue is quite rough. This roughness helps to pull the meat from bones when he's eating, and to clean his coat when he's washing himself.

Smells are very important to kittens—in fact, they probably get as much information through their noses as you get through your eyes. But when out hunting, they use their eyes and ears more than their noses to lead them to their prey.

Every hair on your kitten has a nerve ending, which makes him very sensitive to touch. That's why he likes being petted. These hairs fall out and grow again in Spring and Autumn. He also has tough hairs, called vibrissae, which are permanent. These are in his whiskers, on his cheeks, over his eyes, and in his ears. He uses them as very sensitive feelers, and you should take care never to damage them.

Your kitten will learn from his mother to keep clean by washing himself, but swallowing hairs can make him ill. To keep him really healthy, groom him daily.

Start off by combing him all over, to remove burrs or other things stuck in his hair. Then comes the part he likes—the brushing. First brush all his hair the wrong way, from tail to head. Then brush it back the right way. Get into the habit of grooming him regularly, a few minutes each day. A note of caution: most cats *hate* water, and it is really never necessary to bathe a cat in soap and water.

A kitten's health is important, so any illness should be treated at once. Take him to a vet immediately if he coughs and sneezes, loses weight and has runny eyes or nose. Those are the symptoms of cat flu (distemper), which is dangerous.

Kittens can be immunised against feline enteritis, the most deadly cat disease. A cat with enteritis has a temperature, is thirsty but can't drink, and won't eat. Once a kitten or cat has enteritis, the sickness is almost always fatal. If a kitten dies from enteritis, immediately clean and disinfect everything he has touched. The disease is highly contagious among cats.

When your kitten is older and is allowed outdoors, he's sure to meet other cats and may catch fleas. You can treat him with pyrethrum spray, which won't harm him. You should also spray his basket and the rooms he's been in, as fleas can drop off him and hop back later. Wash his bedding, too.

He might also catch canker, and start to scratch and rub his head. Pet shops sell powder and lotions to treat this, and daily application soon cures it.

Soon your kitten will become a cat. He will grow up, and change his ways. He won't be as cute any more, but he'll still be beautiful. He may not be as playful or cuddly as he was, but he will have other lovable traits. And although he can be let outdoors with little danger of being lost or hurt, he will still need your care, friendship and protection.

People who abandon pets that have changed from cute kittens to ordinary cats are cruel. It's a mistake to think that a grown cat can look after himself and find his own food. Every city and town has its population of wandering, homeless cats. Some manage to survive, but in what a state! Poor, starved beasts, they live in a man-made jungle—cold, diseased, pitiful.

In every city there are organisations—such as the Royal Society for the Prevention of Cruelty to Animals, the People's Dispensary for Sick Animals, and the Cat's Pro-

Why is the kitten on the opposite page so unhappy? It's because · he's climbed up the post and can't get down again!

Opposite page: A rubbish-filled thicket looks to a kitten like a mysterious world to be explored—under the eyes of mother.
Above: Why isn't this kitten chasing the pigeon? Perhaps he doesn't realise it's a bird!

tection League—which try to care for abandoned cats and unwanted kittens. They find homes for many of the kittens. But most of the grown cats are too ill, or too un-appealing, to find new homes, and they have to be destroyed.

Killing any animal is cruel. But these organisations can't find homes, no matter how hard they try, for every wandering cat. And if the cats are left to roam, they'll live miserable lives and produce unhealthy and unhappy kittens.

How can this situation be stopped? Of course, all the animal protection societies work to persuade people to keep their cats, and not to let them produce litters if the kittens can't be looked after. But every cat owner should be aware of the problem.

Should you let your cat have kittens? Yes, if you can look after them or find homes for them. If not, you should have your kitten neutered before it reaches maturity. For males, the operation can be carried out at the age of three to three and a half months. The operation on females is rather more complicated, and they should be three and a half to four and a half months old. Older cats can also have the same operations.

Apart from preventing the birth of unwanted kittens, these operations have other effects. The neutered cat is a more docile and home-loving pet.

HOW KITTENS BEHAVE

You often hear people remark on kittens' and cats' wonderful sense of balance—how they always land on their feet if they fall or are dropped. While this is not strictly true, they do have very fast reflexes and can move very quickly. In fact the cheetah can run faster than any other creature in the world.

This wonderful movement comes from the way their bodies are put together. A cat's spine is held together by very flexible muscles. This means he can curve, stretch or turn in a way that humans, with their stiffer spines, can't do. Also, cats' shoulders are jointed so they can turn their front legs in almost any direction.

The way he's built helps a cat to turn very rapidly and get his feet beneath him as he falls. It also helps him to hold his balance when walking along a narrow ledge or the top of a fence.

But just because a kitten can often land on his feet in a really remarkable way, it doesn't mean he likes falling or being dropped. For him, falling is as frightening as it is for you. If he falls unexpectedly, he may not turn fast enough to land on his feet. He could be badly hurt or even killed by a hard fall.

Kittens are much better at climbing up trees than they are at getting down again. Going up, they can get a good grip on the bark with their claws. But going down, their claws, which point backward, slide instead of gripping. That's why they'll sit crying and helpless in a tree till someone goes to rescue them.

Kittens are very curious—they want to explore and know about everything they see. But they're cautious, too. They don't rush straight into things. They like to sniff and smell things first. You will notice that your kitten always pauses and sniffs his dish of catfood before he takes a bite, just to make sure it's all right. He recognises you, and other people, by your smell as much as by the look or sound of you.

Cats and kittens have a language of their own. It's the same from one cat to another, and is made up of movements and positions as well as sounds.

They purr when they're warm and comfortable—especially when you pet them. They hiss, snarl, spit and cry when angry or frightened. If a kitten wants to be let outdoors or brought in, he cries in one way. If he wants to be fed, he has a similar cry. But it's

a bit different–a little sharper–and when you get to know your kitten, you should be able to tell the difference.

A kitten who's hurt or badly surprised lets out a quite horrible, frightening yowl. If you've ever accidentally stepped on a cat's tail, or dropped something near one, you'll know the sound!

Cats also have different facial expressions, just like people do. As you can see from the pictures in this book, it is easy to tell when a kitten is frightened, angry, embarrassed, or in pain. One good key is to watch his ears. If they are perked up, and forward, he is all right; if they are flattened, and pointed back, you can tell that he is angry about something.

When a kitten sleeps, he seems to put his whole body and soul into it. Curled up, stretched out, or lying on his back with his front paws on his chest, you can see he's

really relaxed and enjoying himself. Although he sometimes seems to choose odd places to sleep, in fact he always goes for a comfortable spot.

Your kitten may choose to doze curled up in your lap. Of course this shows he likes and trusts you. It also shows he likes warmth and softness.

An astonishing thing about cats is the amount of heat they can take. On a hot summer's day you'll find kittens and cats basking in the sunniest, hottest spot they can find. This love of heat draws them to the hearth, where they'll sit staring, squint-eyed, into the flames, as if day-dreaming.

Kittens can take more heat than you could stand. Touch a kitten who's slumbering close to a fire, and he'll feel so hot that you'd expect his hair to be singed. But he seems to need, or certainly to enjoy, his roasting. If you move him away, he'll probably go right back for more.

But he can overdo it, which can lead to an odd sort of complaint. Your basking kitten will suddenly leap up and want to go outdoors–perhaps to cool off, or just to move about. For a few days afterwards, he'll have shivers and twitches, and his eyes will be slightly squinted. But don't worry. It is not as serious as it seems. His appetite will be all right, and when the few days have passed, he'll be quite well, with no after-effects.

Cats are very dignified creatures. They don't like being laughed at, or made to look silly. With a little encouragement, a kitten will play with anyone. But as he grows up, he becomes more serious. As a grown cat he may play with his owner, but rarely with anyone else. And if something happens to a cat to make you laugh at him, he'll give you a hurt, angry glare, turn his back on you and stalk away. Or go to the corner and sit with his back to you, flicking his tail from side to side.

30

One of a cat's most frequent pastimes—besides sleeping, playing and hunting—is scratching. Scratching regularly helps keep his claws in perfect condition by pulling off the outer shells when they become too worn. It also helps keep the muscles and tendons which control the claws in good condition. If you are not careful, your kitten will start to claw the upholstery on your sofas and chairs, so the best thing to do is to teach him to use a special 'cat scratcher'. This is a piece of solid board covered in carpeting material, which you can buy at a pet shop. Place your kitten's paws on it, and he will soon learn to use it instead of the furniture for his claw sharpening activities.

If a cat's claws are so sharp, you may wonder, why don't they make scraping noises on the floor when he walks, and ruin his stealthy movements? This is because they are 'retractile'–they can be pulled in when he does not need them for climbing or grasping prey. When your kitten is playing, he soon learns to keep his claws in so that he doesn't hurt anyone by mistake. Sometimes he can even hurt himself by scratching himself with a claw which has become split or torn. If your kitten damages a claw, the best thing to do is take him to a vet.

KITTENS AND OTHER CREATURES

Kittens are different from cats, in the same way that babies are different from adults. They are more friendly but at the same time more timid than adult cats. They still need a lot of attention and protection—either by their mothers or their owners—from the results of silly actions. A kitten might, for example, run into the road in front of a car, only because he hadn't yet learnt that traffic was dangerous. Or he might make friends with a bird instead of trying to catch and eat it, simply because his mother hadn't yet taught him to hunt.

Most cats chase birds and mice. It's their nature, so you mustn't think that a cat is nasty or bad if he drags a poor dead bird into the house. If you punish him, he simply won't understand. In fact, cats catch far more rodents than birds. And without them we would soon be overrun with rats and mice. A few cats are just not interested in chasing and hunting. Then there are a few who are always trying, but never seem to succeed. But you mustn't laugh at a cat like this or you will offend his dignity and he'll go off and sulk for hours.

Have you seen a mother cat teaching her kittens to hunt? She makes them stay quiet, lurking in hiding with her. A bird flies to earth nearby. The cat stares at the bird with a steady, hungry glare. She crouches close to the ground and creeps towards it. She pauses, raises her rump, shakes it sideways and up and down for two or three seconds, crouches and pounces! Then she lifts her catch in her mouth, proudly carries it back, and gives it to the kittens. Do they learn from this? Stay, and you'll see the kittens practising their stalking and pouncing.

If there's no real bird or mouse to practise on, kittens are quite happy pretending that a stick, a toy mouse, or a piece of paper on a string is the real thing. They also

Above: The crawfish has brought out the hunter instinct in
this kitten.
Opposite page: Most kittens, like this Chinchilla, are fascinated
by the movement of goldfish.

love to leap about the house or garden after any flies and other insects they may spot.

Kittens who haven't been taught to hunt, or who aren't interested, or are too young to feel the hunting urge, have been known to make friends with pet or part-tamed garden birds. But don't be misled into trusting a grown cat with a bird!

Cats and dogs often make friends, if they're raised together. It's a charming sight to find them sitting or playing together. The easiest way to introduce a kitten to a dog, or vice-versa, is in small doses. Until they are accustomed to the company of one another, it is best not to leave these two 'natural enemies' alone together.

If the dog is an adult, then let him into the room where your kitten sleeps—when the kitten is in another room—and let him sniff the bedding. After this, put the kitten down on the floor and let the dog sniff the kitten. With several introductory sessions, the two should eventually make good friends. If the dog gets out of hand, no doubt the kitten will give him a good scratch on the muzzle—proving who's boss!

The main thing to remember is that dogs and cats can be good friends; it only requires time and patience on the part of the owner.

Opposite page: Young animals raised together will be good
friends, like this Persian kitten and the Cocker pups.
Above: The duckling thinks the water is fine, so why is the
kitten complaining about it?

The most important other creatures to a kitten are people. Most kittens like all the attention and petting they can get. How much they want when they grow up depends partly on their owners, but even more on the cat. Some breeds of cats need more attention than others. But within a breed different individuals' needs vary, depending on their own unique personalities.

Some people complain that their cats aren't really friendly animals, like dogs. They tend to treat their home like a hotel, coming in only to demand food or a place to sleep. Well, all cats like to keep a certain feeling of independence. But even the ones who seem most self-reliant really do need their homes. They just don't like to show it.

If a grown-up pulled a cat's tail or ears, or otherwise handled it roughly, he'd be

risking getting a bad scratch. But if a baby, who didn't know he was hurting the cat, did the same thing, the cat would put up with it.

This is because the cat can tell if the hurt is deliberate or not. Nevertheless, a baby should not be allowed to play with a cat–especially not with a kitten–unless someone older is watching. Although it is unlikely that a cat or kitten would hurt a small child, the child might accidentally pull its tail or harm it in some other way, without realising what he was doing.

Perhaps you've heard people say, 'The kitten is so good playing with the baby!' You can be sure that means the kitten is long-suffering, and that the child has not been taught to treat a kitten gently at all times.

A KITTEN'S WORLD

Kittens and cats have all sorts of interests besides eating, sleeping and hunting. They are pleasure-loving creatures and can be not only affectionate but extremely playful.

Smell gives felines a lot of pleasure. To humans, catmint is a dull, uninteresting plant. But kittens and cats go mad for it. Its smell puts them into a state of bliss. So, if you love your kitten, plant some catmint in your garden or in a window-box. If you can't manage that, then buy him a toy mouse, stuffed with dried catmint. He will eat catmint (and probably get sick afterwards, but this helps get rid of hairballs in his tummy and throat), roll in it, kick it around and generally make a mess of your floor. But watching him enjoy himself will probably make up for having to sweep up.

Catmint is so loved by cats that lion trainers use it to calm their animals. Trappers use its concentrated essence to lure pumas and bobcats, who often are a menace around farms, killing sheep and chickens and other animals.

Although cats do not bury bones and food as dogs do, they enjoy digging in loose earth. It upsets a gardener when a kitten uses his flower-bed for a toilet. The kitten seems to think all the lovely earth has been dug up just to make life easy for him. He has no idea that he might be digging up plants!

But the same angry gardener would be charmed to see a kitten appreciating his flowers. Have you ever seen a cat or kitten wandering about a garden, sniffing the flowers with every sign of enjoying their perfume? Cats also like the smell of some women's cosmetics and perfumes.

Smell is not the only enjoyable sense to a cat or kitten. They are creatures of comfort, and they enjoy lolling on soft fabrics. Velvet, soft wools, brocades and other materials will attract them. Of course, they might also sharpen their claws on your

Opposite page: The show-off climbing up the building bricks is a long-haired Tortoiseshell-and-white kitten.
Above: The one up a tree is a Persian.

41

All the kittens on these two pages are tabbies. The studious
one with the book is called a blotched tabby, because his
colour is in splodges. The one clad in a hat is a striped tabby,
because her colour is in lines or bars.

best chair (covered in velvet!), but that is a hazard every cat owner must face.

A sense of fun is one of a cat's or kitten's most delightful qualities. A kitten will enjoy playing with many different objects. Crumpled paper, especially the cellophane from a cigarette packet, will amuse a kitten for hours. Balls of aluminium foil are fun for him to pounce on. Some kittens like climbing into paper bags, for the fun of battling their way out again.

Kittens love to play hide and seek, and a favourite game is to bury themselves in sheets of newspaper. They will peek out from underneath the corners, tentatively stick a paw out and quickly retrieve it, and enjoy frolicking and creating a crisp, crackling, scary–to a kitten–noise.

William Wordsworth, the famous English poet, wrote about 'The Kitten Playing with the Fallen Leaves':

> See the kitten on the wall
> Sporting with the leaves that fall! . . .
> —But the kitten how she starts!
> Crouches, stretches, paws, and darts:
> First at one, and then its fellow,
> Just as light, and just as yellow . . .

All in all, cats and kittens lead busy and active lives—individual lives. Some cats are music lovers, and will sit for hours listening to the wireless, or to a violin or piano. Other cats enjoy the wind or listening to and watching the rain beat against a window pane.

One thing is sure about kittens and cats, if they are certain of their owner's love, then they will be the most relaxed, affectionate and amusing pets in the animal kingdom.

43

FEAR AND FEROCITY

When a kitten is frightened, he behaves in a well-known, but nevertheless startling, manner. First he crouches flat on the ground, as if about to leap. Then he straightens up and makes himself look as frightening as possible. His hair bristles all over, so that he seems very much bigger, and quite fierce. His tail, with every hair sticking straight out, looks like a great bottle brush. It thrashes about fiercely. His eyes glare, his ears flatten backwards, and his mouth opens wide to show all his sharp teeth. He makes horrible sounds—yowls, hisses and spits. Even in a kitten this behaviour can be frightening enough to make large dogs and some people back off. A badly startled pugnacious-looking cat can really be quite daunting. None but the very brave, or very foolish, would attempt to battle with him.

If he is then attacked, a kitten does one of two things. He runs to safety if he can. If trapped, he attacks like lightning with claws extended to scratch.

Many things besides the possibility of attack frighten a kitten. Sudden noises, either loud or sharp, will bring him leaping and hissing out of the deepest slumber. Animals or people he doesn't like, or sudden nasty smells, will set him to twitching, growling or complaining, sometimes ready to fight.

A cat has two areas which he considers belong to him. The first, and very personal area, is his lair. It could be his sleeping basket, or the centre of the hearth-rug, or a particular chair. At any rate, he will defend his right to it against any other cat, and is prepared to fight for it if necessary.

His second area is his territory, indoors and out. This usually contains other cats. In any territory there is one boss or dictator cat, with all his followers. When several cats share the same territory, they get on much better than a group of dogs would do, once they've decided who's boss. The decision is made by fighting. But the boss cat in any territory is not necessarily the biggest or youngest, he is simply the one—male or female—who can dominate all the others.

Let a new cat come into the territory and the boss cat immediately confronts him. He arches his back and glares. If that doesn't frighten the intruder, the dictator points his tail straight up and raises the hair on it. His claws come out, ready to attack. A

45

Above: A frightened kitten—he's scared of falling!
Opposite page: The battle looks fierce, with teeth and claws flashing—but the kittens are really playing.

cowardly newcomer will back down. A brave one will prepare to fight. Finally, they spit and hiss, and, if neither is frightened off, they fight. When one is frightened or ready to give in, he submits by flattening himself against the ground. Then the winner stands over the loser for a few seconds, holding him by the skin of his neck. He doesn't hurt the loser by doing this, it's simply a way of marking, once and for all, that he's the top cat in that territory.

Cats living together in the same house are not usually great friends. They just put up with one another for the sake of peace and quiet. In a litter of kittens there is often a 'boss' kitten, who gets his way by being stronger and able to push the others away from what he wants. Although they sometimes appear to fight, kittens are only playing, and get along together quite happily for their first three months or so.

Cats have been pets for many centuries. We know that the first people to domesticate the cat were probably the Egyptians. Grain was an important crop in ancient Egypt, and cats being naturally good ratters no doubt gained the approval and later the affection of the Egyptians. There is a drawing of a cat wearing a lotus blossom collar in an Egyptian tomb which dates back to 2600 B.C., so cats have had a prominent place in society for thousands of years.

But who were the cat's ancestors? Scientists are almost certain that the cat developed from a family of animals called *Miacidae*, which lived about 50 million years ago. *Miacidae* were meat-eating, ugly looking, weasel-like creatures.

After about 14 million years, a branch of the *Miacidae* family developed called the *Dinictis*. This creature was much more like the cat of today. It had a body about the size of a lynx, cat-like teeth, and claws which could extend and retract.

Then, during the last million years of the Stone Age, when man's ancestors first appeared on earth, *Felis catus*, our domestic cat, began to thrive.

Since then, the physical characteristics of the pet cat have changed little. And while

Above: Two kittens wait patiently at the
back door for some milk.
At right: Setting off to explore the miniature
jungle of the back garden.

a visitor from outer space might not recognise that an Alsatian dog and a Pekinese were from the same family, he would have little trouble seeing that a Siamese cat and a Scottish wild cat were relations.

Cats have been treated in very different ways by different peoples and nations. At first, the Egyptians used cats to catch rats in their storehouses, and then the animal became a symbol of friendliness. Later, the cat was looked to as a goddess of the home, a symbol of femininity, and was called Pasht or Bastet. This goddess had the body of a woman and the head of a cat.

Later, when the Romans conquered Egypt, the story goes that a Roman soldier accidentally killed a cat. Accident or not, this so enraged the local people that they killed him and rebelled against Rome. The rebellion covered the country and led to the deaths of Antony and Cleopatra in the end.

Throughout history, cats have been the subject of legends in many lands. Mohammed, the great Muslim prophet, is supposed to have had a pet cat called Muezza. One day, so as not to disturb the cat, who was sleeping on his arm, Mohammed cut off his sleeve. Later, when he came back, the cat bowed to thank him. So Mohammed stroked the cat three times. With this miraculous touch, Mohammed gave the cat and all its descendants the ability to land on their feet whenever they fell.

In Japan, so legend says, in the year 999, a cat gave birth to five blue-eyed white kittens in the Emperor's palace. The Emperor was so impressed that he ordered that the kittens should be treated like princes. Centuries passed, and Japan was full of cats, all still regarded as princes. It was impossible for the Japanese to ask their princely beasts to catch mice for them, although mice had become a terrible nuisance, preying on the silkworms which supplied cocoons to the Japanese silk makers. They tried to scare off the mice by making paintings and statues of cats, but the mice paid no attention to the images. At last the mice became so bad that a law was passed saying that all cats must be set loose. The cats stopped being princes, but they became very good mousers!

'Somebody rescue me!' this kitten cries.

Today there is a Buddhist temple in Tokyo consecrated to the cat. In the temple–Go-To-Ku-Ji–are thousands of statues and images of beckoning cats, nearly all of them shown with their right front paw raised beside their faces. They represent Maneki-Neko, an enchanted cat who can summon good luck and happiness. All round the temple are the graves of well-loved pet cats, and in the temple are priests who pray for the cats' souls.

In the Middle Ages in Europe, when there were plagues of rats, cats were highly valued as rat catchers. Howell Dda, Prince of Aberfraw in Wales, passed some very strict laws concerning cats in the tenth century. He decreed that a good ratting cat was worth a foal, a calf or a pig. A cat which caught a mouse doubled its own value. Someone buying a cat had the right to expect that it was in good health, and that a female cat could produce and properly care for kittens. If someone stole or killed another person's cat, the fine was a pile of corn big enough to cover the cat when held by its tail with its nose touching the ground.

At the time of the Crusades, black rats slipped into Europe in the ships of returning Crusaders. Soon there were millions of rats infesting the continent. More and more cats were called for–many of them also brought back from the Near East in Crusader

Kitten emotions. *From left to right:* An angry kitten arches his back and spits. A wet and unhappy character cries for help. A startled kitten leaps to the alert.

ships. The cats eventually brought the rats under control, and succeeded in making themselves very popular. But they became, in a way, too popular with the wrong people. They were made a symbol of a pagan cult which worshipped the goddess Freya, and this brought down on them the wrath of the Christian church. Cats were persecuted as devils. Even the people who befriended cats were persecuted. They were accused of being witches, and cats were considered their go-betweens with the Devil. Many people—and cats—were burned at the stake.

Cats have always been the subject of superstitions and sayings. How many times have you heard that 'curiosity killed the cat' or that 'cats have nine lives'? In Britain it is considered lucky if a black cat crosses your path, but in America it is believed to be an ill omen. In South America, black cats are considered so evil that they can cause disease and even death.

THE SIXTH SENSE

Pet kittens and cats can sometimes give the impression that they find life with humans very boring and uninteresting. They'll yawn, and wander off to stare into the distance, day-dreaming or seeing something that we mere humans can't.

Much has been said about cats' famous sixth sense. They seem somehow to be able to sense things that are about to happen, or things we cannot detect.

What makes a peaceful cat suddenly leap up, showing every sign of fear, when nothing has happened? Do cats feel the presence of ghosts or danger? During the Second World War, many people claimed that their cats knew when bombs were about to be dropped. And there are many tales of cats who won't go near a spot where someone has met with a violent death. What do they see or feel? No one knows, and no one has been able to verify this 'sixth sense' scientifically.

There is one such strange quality in cats which has been studied. It's their astonishing ability to find their way home from a completely unknown place without the help of any signs that we can understand. Some German scientists experimented by shutting cats in boxes so they couldn't see where they were going. They were taken a long way from home, and released in a maze which had twenty-four exits. Eight out of ten cats left the maze by the exit closest to their homes! The cats who hesitated longest, or chose the wrong exits, were always very young cats. The farther they were from home, the more mistakes they made.

There are many stories of cats who have found their way home over hundreds of miles. One of the most astonishing is the story of a cat who tracked his master from their old home to a new home right across the American continent. The cat was left in New York when his owner, a veterinarian, moved across the United States to California. Five months later the cat entered his new house, climbed on to the armchair that had always been its favourite, and fell asleep. Although the cat looked and behaved exactly like the one he'd left behind, the veterinarian could hardly believe his eyes—until he remembered that his cat had had an accident which left it with an enlarged bone in its spine. He felt the newcomer, and there was the same large bone. It was the same cat, who had crossed the United States to be with its master!

BREEDS

There are many breeds of cats which have been developed for a particular appearance. These are usually very beautiful. Some, like the Rex and Peke-faced cats, seem to be admired as much because they're different as because they're fine-looking animals.

Cats come in three main groups: Some short-haired breeds are well-made and powerful, with deep chests and broad heads. Other short-haired breeds—like the Siamese—are lighter in build, with fine, pointed faces. Long-haired breeds, such as Angoras or Persians, have beautiful, silky hair, broad heads, heavy bodies and short legs.

These are some of the types and breeds:

Blacks: You might think there were plenty of these about, but very few would win prizes at shows. They must have all-black hairs, with not a single white one, and they must have orange eyes. Most black cats have green or greenish eyes.

Whites: A few have blue eyes, which is very pretty with pure white hair, but they're often deaf. Most have golden-orange or copper coloured eyes.

Blues: These are very popular, having blue-grey hair and big yellow eyes.

Tortoiseshells: They have black, light red and dark red patches all over, with no white hairs. The Tortoiseshell-and-white are the same, but with white hairs added. Japanese sailors are keen on Tortoiseshell-and-white cats, because they believe the cats bring good luck. They keep off the spirits of the deep and prevent shipwrecks—or so the sailors say!

Tabbies: There are all kinds. Some have blotches, some have stripes, some have very fine stripes and are called mackerel tabbies, and some have spots. They can be brown, grey, silver or red in shading.

Manx: These have no tails or very short stubs of tails and come from the Isle of Man. Although there are cats without tails in other parts of the world, the Manx doesn't seem to have any close relatives.

According to legend, the Manx cat has no tail because he was the last animal into Noah's Ark, and got his tail cut off when the door closed.

For show purposes, the ideal Manx cat has no sign of a tail at all, but only a little hollow where his tail should be, and a rump as round as an orange. His long hind legs make his rump stick up and give him a rather rabbity, hopping movement. His coat also looks very much like a rabbit's and can be any colour.

Abyssinian: Despite its name, this is a British-bred cat. It has a ruddy brown or light red coat, with two or three bars of colour (called ticking) on each hair.

Siamese: Nearly everyone adores these beautiful cats. Their usual colour is cream with dark brown markings, called points. But Siamese can be ivory with chocolate brown points, white with blue, off-white with frosty grey, and even white with gold.

Rex: Any kind of cat, long-haired or short, can have a rex-type coat. Each hair is slightly curled and shortish, so the cat looks as if he's had a permanent wave.

Burmese: This is a fairly new breed, created by the School of Genetics at Harvard University. (The Burmese is not the same as the Birman.) The first cats bred to create the Burmese were a brown cat from Burma, Wong Mau, and a Siamese. Their kittens were half and half. Over many generations, the desired characteristics were worked for until the breed became self-perpetuating. That means that two Burmese will now produce kittens like themselves. The Burmese has the shape of a Siamese, except that its tail is a bit thicker and shorter, and the ears are shorter, too. It has beautiful

Below: A Chinchilla.
Opposite page: The strange-looking cat at the top is a Peke-faced Persian. The one in the lower right hand corner is a Himalayan, a Persian with Siamese markings. Compare them with the ordinary kitten in the lower left-hand corner.

This is an Abyssinian, a breed which is more friendly and wants
more attention than most cats.

yellow Oriental eyes and short, dark brown hair. Burmese kittens have paler hair, and
dark Siamese markings show on them for a time.

Even more recent is the Blue Burmese. He looks the same as a Brown Burmese,
except that his coat is blue-grey, with paler grey or light brown on his belly.

Birman: Another unusual breed is the Birman, also called the Sacred Cat of Burma.
Its markings are similar to the Siamese, but its body is heavier, its hair is long, and a
golden-fawn colour. The thing that makes it really different from the Siamese and the
Colourpoint is its feet, which are all pure white.

Persians: These long-haired cats, also known as Angoras, were introduced to Europe
in about 1550, but today look quite different from their original ancestors. They have
been bred to have large, strong bodies, round heads with big eyes and small noses,
great ruffs of silky hair, and very fluffy tails. They come in many colours, and breeders
all over the world compete to produce cats in new colours and combinations of colour.
They're the beautiful, pampered aristocrats of the cat world.

The greatest difficulty that breeders of these cats have is to get their coats exactly
right. White Persians sometimes have yellowish coats, which are considered poor at
the cat shows. Others have fine, beautifully silky white fur, but their owners have
great trouble keeping them clean, especially their tails.

For show purposes, a black Persian must have a perfectly inky coat. The trouble is,
you can't tell how a kitten will turn out until he's about six months old. Black kittens
go rusty coloured, while rusty kittens may eventually have the best coats! Sunlight

Manx kittens. They're a breed from the Isle of Man which are
born without tails.

can turn a black's coat rusty, and even washing too much will fade his coat!

The fiercest-looking pet cat is the Long-Haired (or Persian) Red Tabby. He has
bright red stripes on a paler colour, and what with that and his great bright eyes and
enormous ruff, he looks more like a mini jungle beast than a pet. Yet, like all the
Persians, he is a gentle, charming companion.

Chinchillas: These are a bit finer in build than other long-haired cats, which suits
their delicate colouring very well. The Chinchilla has a pure white undercoat, and a
white topcoat where the hairs are just tipped with black. This gives him a shimmering,
silvery appearance, especially as his chin, chest, belly and ear tufts are pure white.
He has big beautiful blue or emerald green eyes. Some Chinchilla kittens are born with
ringed tails or barred legs. These sometimes disappear, but the anxious owners won't
know for sure until the kittens are about ten weeks old.

Now that you know something about kittens, how to take care of them, what kind of
breeds there are, and how they behave, you may wish to own one.

Kittens are truly the most lovable of pets. They will reward you with hours of
affection and amusement in return for gentle care and concern.

Perhaps the best and last word on kittens and cats should be left to the cat lover
and humorist Mark Twain, who wrote, 'If man could be crossed with the cat, it would
improve man, but deteriorate the cat.'

60